▶Thinking Basics

**Comprehension A
Workbook**

Siegfried Engelmann • Phyllis Haddox • Susan Hanner • Jean Osborn

**SRA
McGraw-Hill**

Columbus, Ohio

A Division of The McGraw·Hill Companies

SRA/McGraw-Hill

*A Division of The **McGraw·Hill** Companies*

2002 Imprint
Copyright © 1999 by SRA/McGraw-Hill.

Send all inquiries to:
SRA/McGraw-Hill
8787 Orion Place
Columbus, OH 43240-4027

Printed in the United States of America.

ISBN 0-02-674801-0

11 12 13 14 POH 07 06 05

A

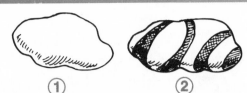

①   ②   ③   ④   ⑤

B

C

①   ②   ③   ④

D

①   ②   ③

All _____.   Fido _____.   So, _____.

E

LESSON B

A

B

① ② ③ ④ ⑤

C

① ② ③

D

① ② ③ ④

E

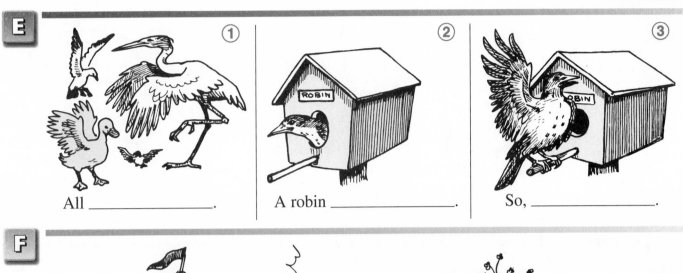

① All _____.

② A robin _____.

③ So, _____.

F

1	2		TOTAL

A

B

①   ②   ③   ④   ⑤

C

①   ②   ③   ④

D

①   ②   ③

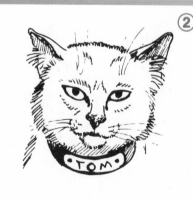

All _____.

Tom _____.

So, _____.

E

F

① ② ③ ④ ⑤

LESSON D

A

B

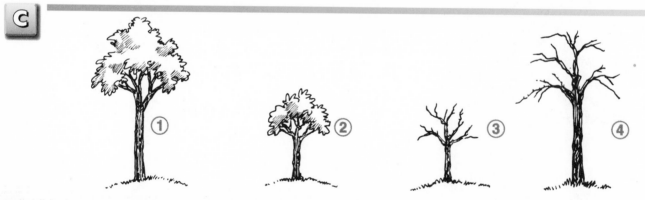

C

① ② ③ ④

D

① ② ③

All _____.   A trout _____.   So, _____.

A

B

C

① ② ③ ④

D

① ② ③

E

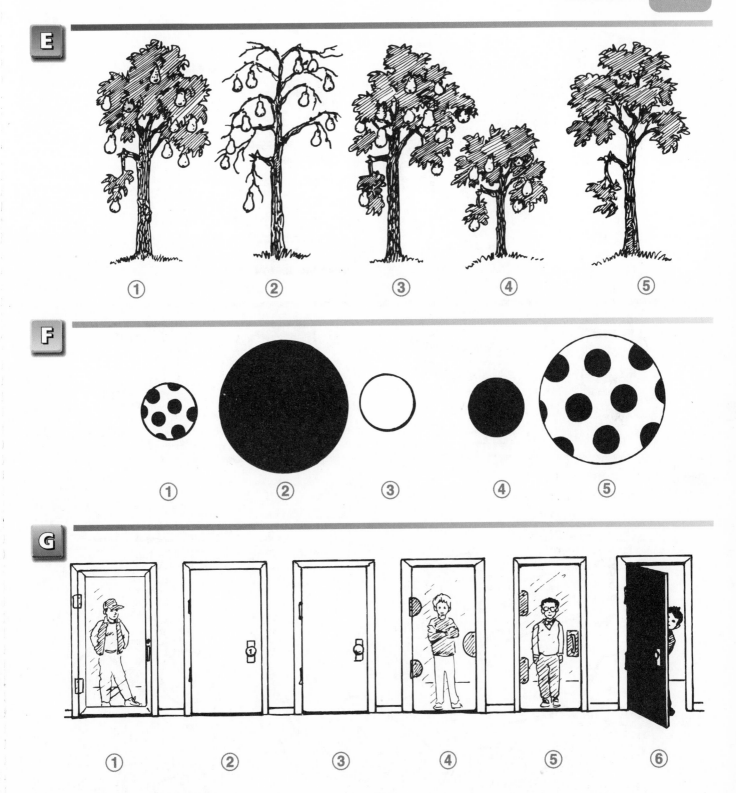

① ② ③ ④ ⑤

F

① ② ③ ④ ⑤

G

① ② ③ ④ ⑤ ⑥

LESSON 1

A

B

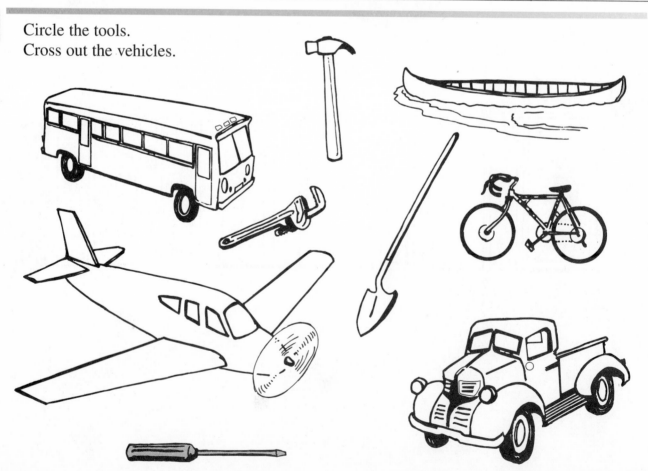

| **1.** true   false | **2.** true   false | **3.** true   false | **4.** true   false |

C

Circle the tools.
Cross out the vehicles.

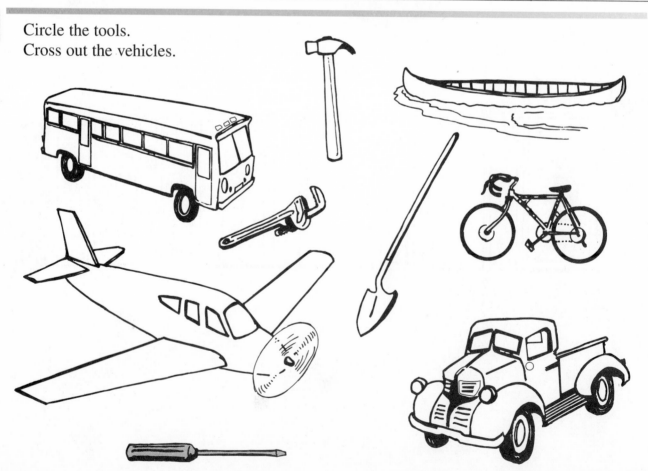

1	2	3	4

TOTAL

A

B

1. true false	**2.** true false	**3.** true false	**4.** true false

C

1. true false	**2.** true false	**3.** true false	**4.** true false

D

Underline the containers.
Circle the animals.

1	2	3	4		TOTAL

A

① ② ③

B

C

1. true false	**2.** true false	**3.** true false	**4.** true false	**5.** true false

D

Cross out the foods.
Underline the buildings.

E

ⓐ ⓑ ⓒ

1. _____
2. _____
3. _____

A

①  ②  ③

B

Make a box around the furniture.
Circle the plants.

C

1. _____
2. _____
3. _____

ⓐ   ⓑ   ⓒ

D

E

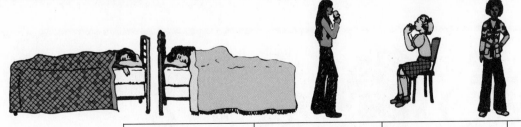

| 1. true   false | 2. true   false | 3. true   false | 4. true   false |

1	2	3	4		TOTAL

A

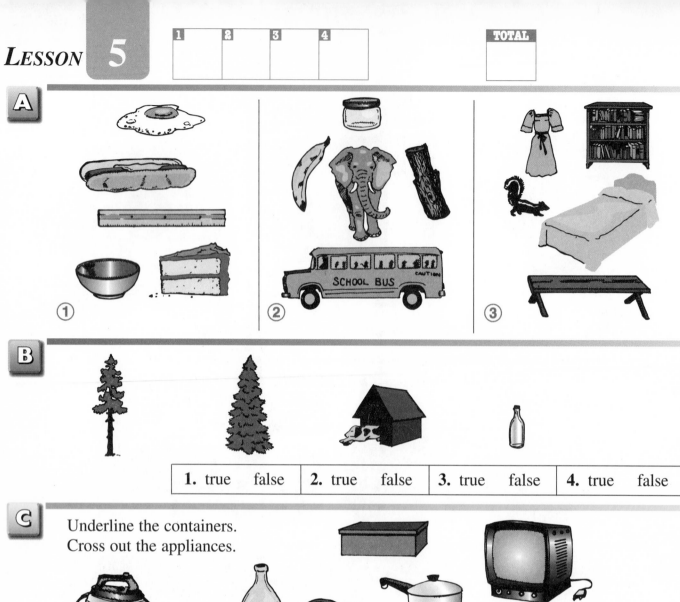

① ② ③

B

1. true false	**2.** true false	**3.** true false	**4.** true false

C

Underline the containers.
Cross out the appliances.

D

1. _____
2. _____
3. _____

E

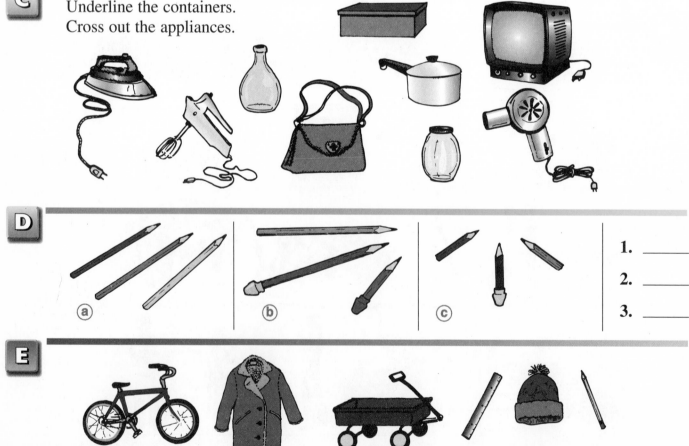

A

1. _____

2. _____

3. _____

B

1. _____

2. _____

3. _____

C

Circle the tools.
Underline the animals.

D

| 1. true   false | 2. true   false | 3. true   false | 4. true   false |

E

① ② ③

LESSON 7

1	2	3	4		TOTAL

A

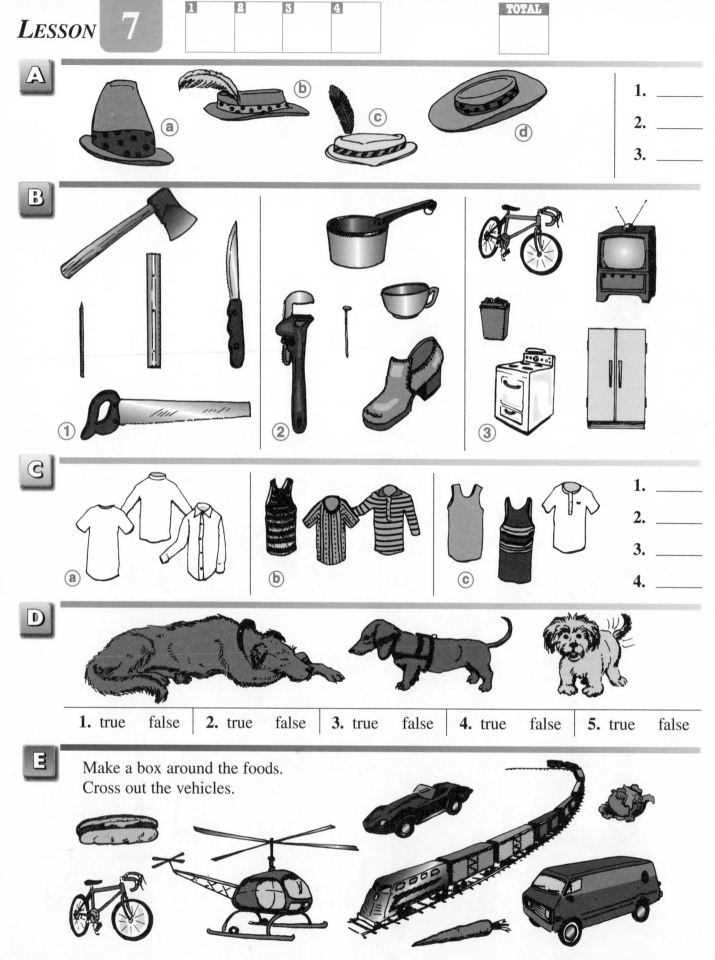

1. _____
2. _____
3. _____

B

C

1. _____
2. _____
3. _____
4. _____

D

1. true false	2. true false	3. true false	4. true false	5. true false

E

Make a box around the foods.
Cross out the vehicles.

A

① ② ③

B

Cross out the buildings.
Circle the furniture.

C

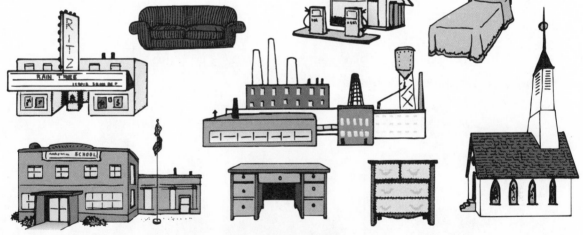

1. true   false | **2.** true   false | **3.** true   false | **4.** true   false | **5.** true   false

D

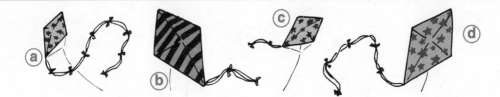

ⓐ ⓑ ⓒ ⓓ

1. _____
2. _____
3. _____

1	2	3	4

TOTAL

A

Make a box around the plants.
Underline the appliances.

   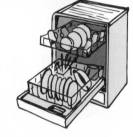

B

  (a)   (b)   (c)   (d)

1. _____

2. _____

3. _____

C

① ② ③

D

1. true false	2. true false	3. true false	4. true false	5. true false

A

B

①

②

③

C

ⓐ   ⓑ   ⓒ

1. _____
2. _____
3. _____
4. _____

D

Underline the vehicles.
Cross out the tools.

E

1. true false	**2.** true false	**3.** true false	**4.** true false	**5.** true false

1	2	3	4		TOTAL

A

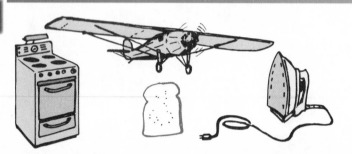

1. true   false   maybe

2. true   false   maybe

3. true   false   maybe

4. true   false   maybe

5. true   false   maybe

B

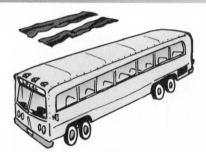

C

①

②

③

D

Circle the foods.
Make a box around the buildings.

1	2	3	4		TOTAL

A

1. true	false	maybe
2. true	false	maybe
3. true	false	maybe
4. true	false	maybe

B

Underline the furniture.
Make a box around the containers.

C

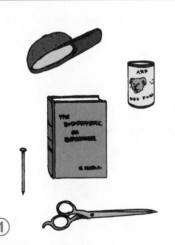

① ② ③

D

| 1. _____ |
| 2. _____ |
| 3. _____ |
| 4. _____ |

ⓒ ⓓ ⓔ

E

| 1. _____ |
| 2. _____ |
| 3. _____ |

ⓐ ⓑ ⓒ ⓓ

1	2	3	4		TOTAL

A Cross out the plants.
Underline the foods.

B

1. true   false   maybe
2. true   false   maybe
3. true   false   maybe
4. true   false   maybe
5. true   false   maybe

C

ⓐ   ⓑ   ⓒ   ⓓ

1. _____
2. _____
3. _____

D

①

②

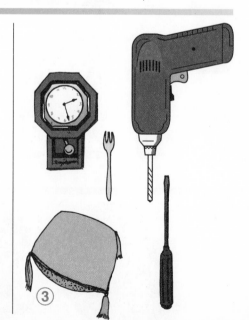

③

A

B

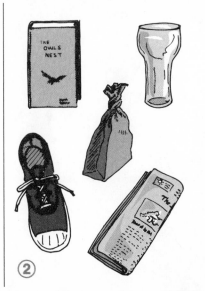

1. true   false   maybe

2. true   false   maybe

3. true   false   maybe

4. true   false   maybe

C

① ② ③

D

Circle the appliances.
Make a box around the vehicles.

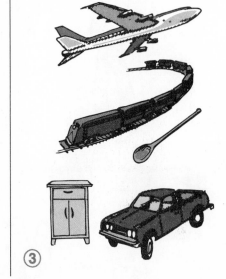

1	2	3	4		TOTAL

A

Cross out the furniture.
Underline the containers.

B

1. true	false	maybe
2. true	false	maybe
3. true	false	maybe
4. true	false	maybe

C

D

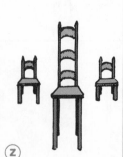

1. _____

2. _____

3. _____

4. _____

ⓧ   ⓨ   ⓩ

A

B

 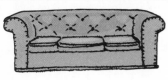  

ⓒ ⓓ ⓔ

1. _____
2. _____
3. _____
4. _____

C

ⓐ ⓑ ⓒ ⓓ

1. _____
2. _____
3. _____

D

1. true   false   maybe

2. true   false   maybe

3. true   false   maybe

4. true   false   maybe

LESSON

A

1. true   false   maybe

2. true   false   maybe

3. true   false   maybe

4. true   false   maybe

B

C

  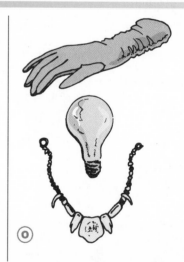

ⓜ   ⓝ   ⓞ

1. _____

2. _____

3. _____

4. _____

D

ⓐ   ⓑ   ⓒ   ⓓ

1. _____

2. _____

3. _____

1	2	3	4		TOTAL

A

B

1. true	false	maybe
2. true	false	maybe
3. true	false	maybe
4. true	false	maybe

C

ⓐ   ⓑ   ⓒ   ⓓ

1. _____
2. _____
3. _____

D

Put an **A** on the vehicles.
Put a **B** on the tools.

1	2	3	4

TOTAL

A

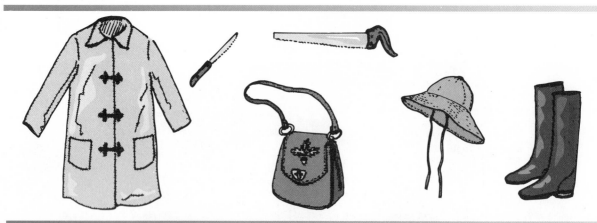

B

1.	true	false	maybe
2.	true	false	maybe
3.	true	false	maybe
4.	true	false	maybe

C

1. _____
2. _____
3. _____

D

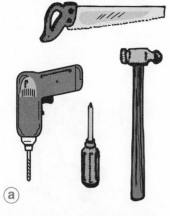

1. _____
2. _____
3. _____
4. _____

1. true	false	maybe	
2. true	false	maybe	
3. true	false	maybe	
4. true	false	maybe	

A

B

(a)

(b)

(c)

1. _____
2. _____
3. _____
4. _____

C

①

②

③

D

1. true	false	maybe
2. true	false	maybe
3. true	false	maybe
4. true	false	maybe

E

1. Pass   Fail   2. Pass   Fail

F

1. Pass   Fail

A

1. true   false   maybe

2. true   false   maybe

3. true   false   maybe

4. true   false   maybe

B

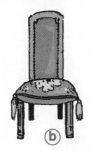

ⓐ   ⓑ   ⓒ   ⓓ

1. _____

2. _____

3. _____

C

D

1. true   false   maybe

2. true   false   maybe

3. true   false   maybe

4. true   false   maybe

5. true   false   maybe

6. true   false   maybe

1	2	3	4		TOTAL

A

B

1.	true	false	maybe
2.	true	false	maybe
3.	true	false	maybe
4.	true	false	maybe
5.	true	false	maybe
6.	true	false	maybe

C

1.	true	false	maybe	**5.**	true	false	maybe
2.	true	false	maybe	**6.**	true	false	maybe
3.	true	false	maybe	**7.**	true	false	maybe
4.	true	false	maybe				

D

(a)   (b)   (c)

1. _____
2. _____
3. _____
4. _____

1	2	3	4		TOTAL

A

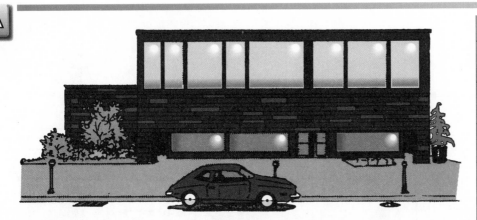

1. true	false	maybe
2. true	false	maybe
3. true	false	maybe
4. true	false	maybe
5. true	false	maybe
6. true	false	maybe

B

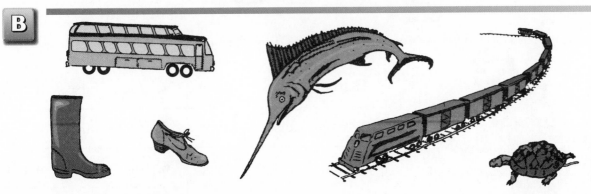

C

1. true	false	maybe
2. true	false	maybe
3. true	false	maybe
4. true	false	maybe
5. true	false	maybe
6. true	false	maybe

D

ⓐ   ⓑ   ⓒ   ⓓ

1. _____
2. _____
3. _____

1	2	3	4

TOTAL

A-1

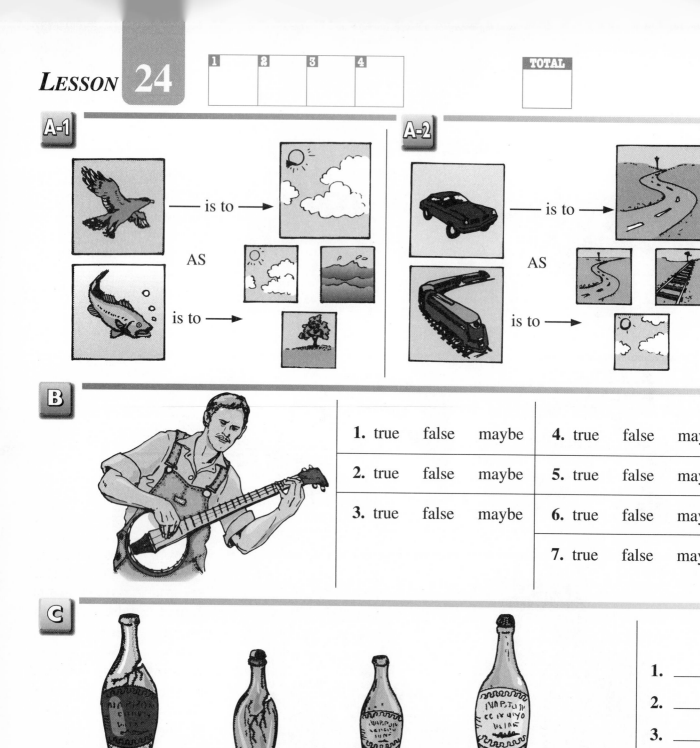

A-2

B

1. true false maybe	4. true false maybe
2. true false maybe	5. true false maybe
3. true false maybe	6. true false maybe
	7. true false maybe

C

ⓐ   ⓑ   ⓒ   ⓓ

1. _____
2. _____
3. _____

D

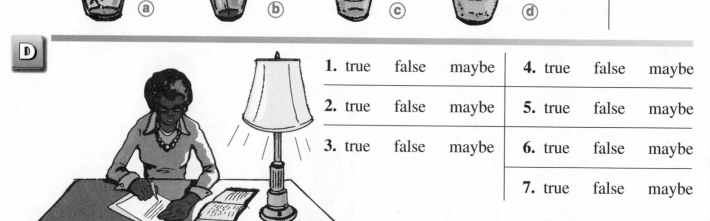

1. true false maybe	4. true false maybe
2. true false maybe	5. true false maybe
3. true false maybe	6. true false maybe
	7. true false maybe

1 2 3 4

TOTAL

A-1

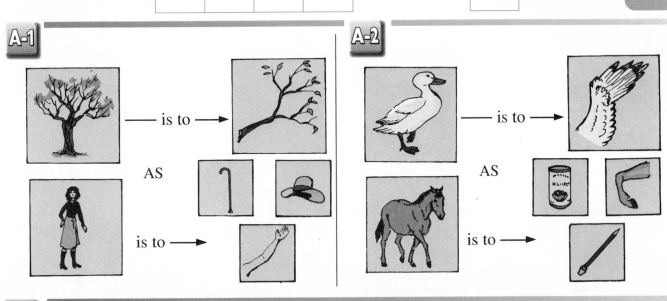

is to →

AS

is to →

A-2

is to →

AS

is to →

B

1. ____

2. ____

3. ____

C

1.	true	false	maybe
2.	true	false	maybe
3.	true	false	maybe
4.	true	false	maybe
5.	true	false	maybe
6.	true	false	maybe

D

ⓐ

ⓑ

ⓒ

E

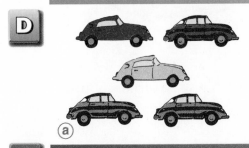

ⓐ

ⓑ

ⓒ

1	2	3	4		TOTAL

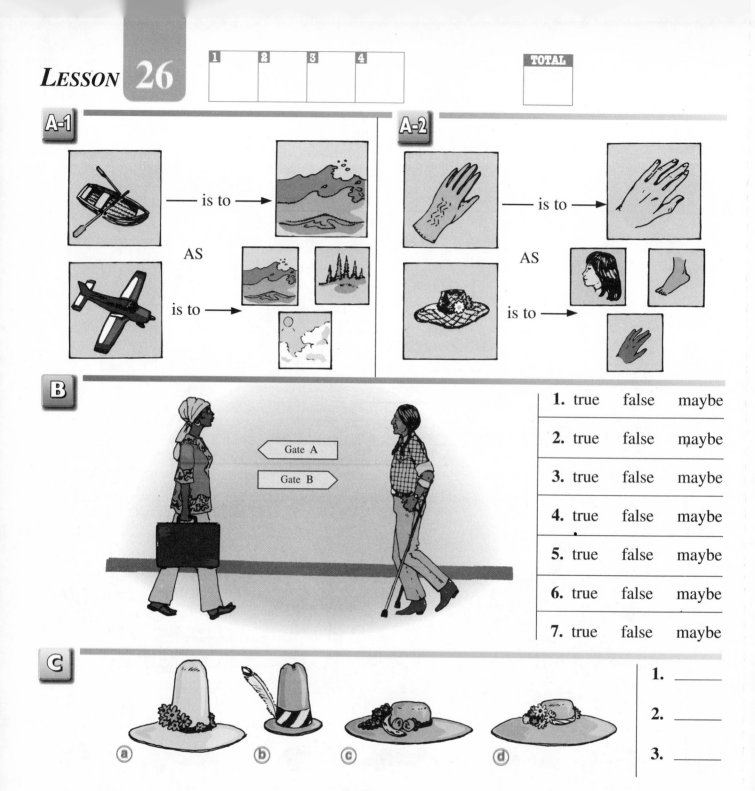

A-1

is to

AS

is to

A-2

is to

AS

is to

B

Gate A

Gate B

1. true   false   maybe
2. true   false   maybe
3. true   false   maybe
4. true   false   maybe
5. true   false   maybe
6. true   false   maybe
7. true   false   maybe

C

ⓐ   ⓑ   ⓒ   ⓓ

1. _____
2. _____
3. _____

D

(a)

(b)

(c)

1. _____
2. _____
3. _____
4. _____

E

(a)

(b)

(c)

F

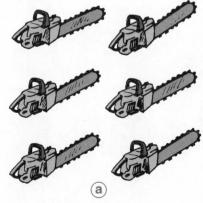

(a)

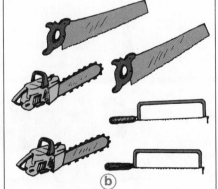

(b)

(c)

1	2	3	4

TOTAL

A

1. true   false   maybe
2. true   false   maybe
3. true   false   maybe
4. true   false   maybe
5. true   false   maybe
6. true   false   maybe

B

C-1

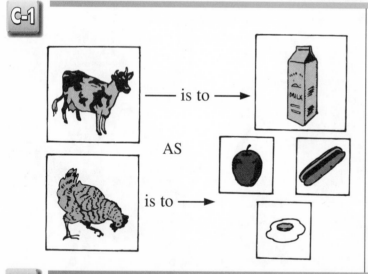

is to

AS

is to

C-2

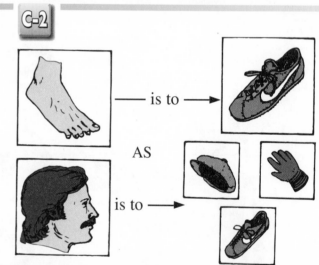

is to

AS

is to

D

ⓐ   ⓑ   ⓒ

E

ⓐ   ⓑ   ⓒ

1	2	3	4

TOTAL

A

1. true	false	maybe
2. true	false	maybe
3. true	false	maybe
4. true	false	maybe
5. true	false	maybe
6. true	false	maybe
7. true	false	maybe

B

ⓐ

ⓑ

ⓒ

1. _____
2. _____
3. _____
4. _____

C-1

 is to →

AS

 is to →

C-2

is to →

AS

 is to →

D

ⓐ   ⓑ   ⓒ   ⓓ

1. _____
2. _____
3. _____

E

F

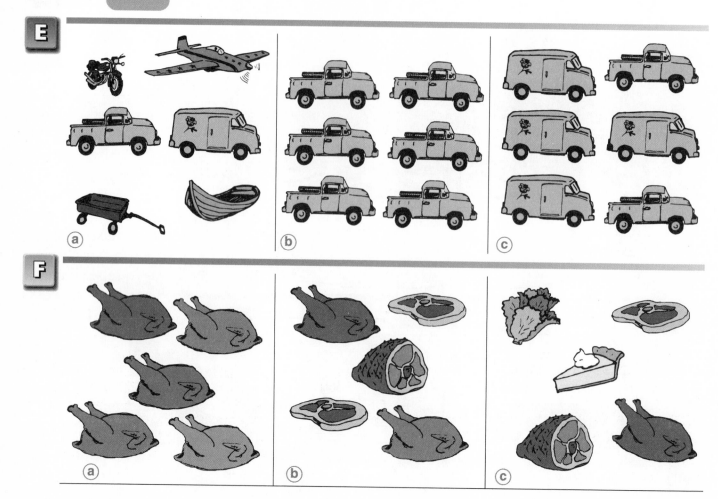

A

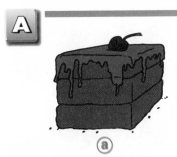
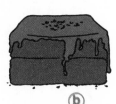

ⓐ ⓑ ⓒ ⓓ

1. _____
2. _____
3. _____

B-1

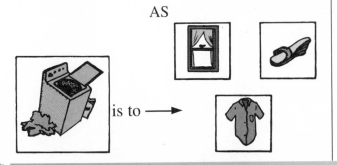

is to →

AS

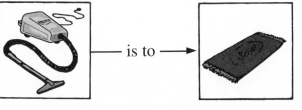

is to →

B-2

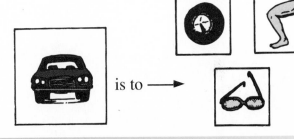

is to →

AS

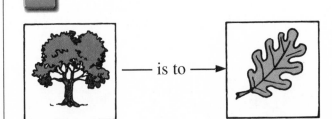

is to →

C

1.	true	false	maybe
2.	true	false	maybe
3.	true	false	maybe
4.	true	false	maybe
5.	true	false	maybe
6.	true	false	maybe

D

ⓐ

ⓑ

ⓒ

A

ⓐ ⓑ ⓒ

A

1.	true	false	maybe
2.	true	false	maybe
3.	true	false	maybe
4.	true	false	maybe
5.	true	false	maybe
6.	true	false	maybe

B

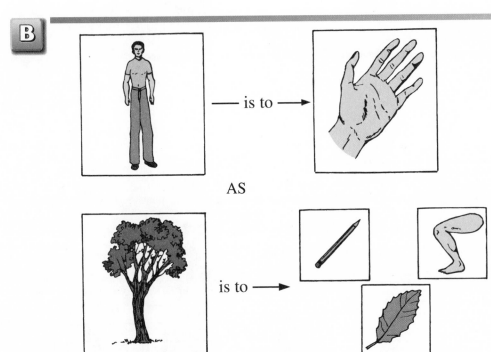

AS

C

ⓐ   ⓑ   ⓒ   ⓓ

1. _____
2. _____
3. _____

D

1. Pass   Fail

E

1. Pass   Fail   **2.** Pass   Fail   **3.** Pass   Fail

1	2	3	4

TOTAL

A

Write true, false, or maybe.

> **Here's the only thing Fred did.**
> **Fred shined the long shoes.**

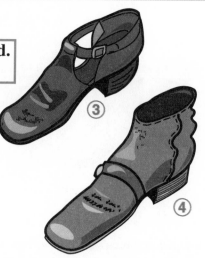

1. Fred shined object 2. _____

2. Fred shined object 3. _____

3. Fred did not shine object 4. _____

B

①   ②   ③   ④   ⑤

C

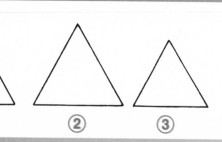

is to   AS   is to

D

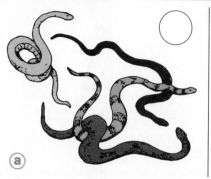

a   b   c

_____   _____   _____

reptiles   striped snakes   snakes

A

Write true, false, or maybe.

> **Here's the only thing Ann did.**
> **Ann built the short tables.**

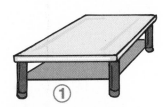

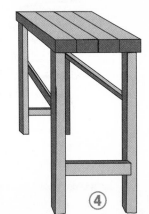

1. Ann built object 2. _____

2. Ann did not build object 3. _____

3. Ann did not build object 4. _____

B

① ② ③ ④ ⑤

C

is to ↓

AS

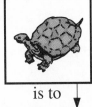
is to ↓

D

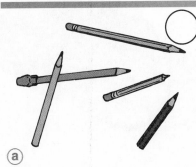 ◯

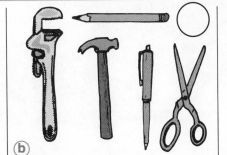 ◯

 ◯

ⓐ _____ ⓑ _____ ⓒ _____

tools   writing tools   pencils

1	2	3	4		TOTAL

A

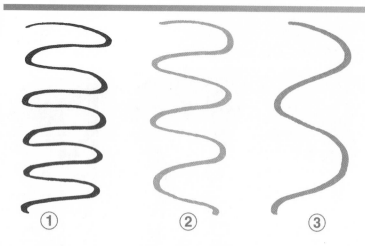

①   ②   ③   ④   ⑤

B

Write true, false, or maybe.

> **Here's the only thing the woman did.**
> **The woman wore some of the tall hats.**

①   ②   ③   ④

1. The woman wore object 1.   _____

2. The woman wore object 4.   _____

3. The woman did not wear object 4. _____

C

Write true, false, or maybe.

> **Here's the only thing the fire did.**
> **The fire burned fat logs.**

④   ②   ③   ①

1. The fire burned object 1.   _____

2. The fire did not burn object 2. _____

3. The fire burned object 3.   _____

D

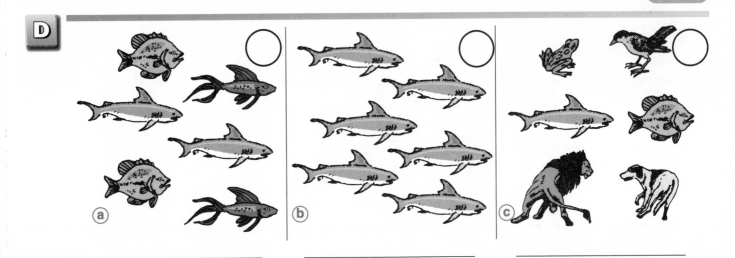

sharks   animals   fish

E

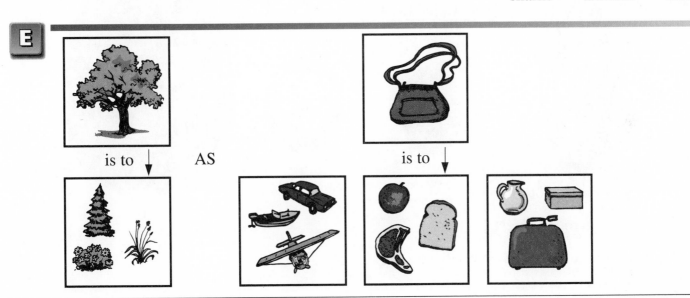

is to   AS   is to

1	2	3	4

TOTAL

A

① ② ③ ④ ⑤

B

Write true, false, or maybe.

> **Here's the only thing Bob did.**
> **Bob rolled the tall wheels.**

① ② ③ ④

1. Bob did not roll object 1. _____

2. Bob rolled object 1. _____

3. Bob did not roll object 4. _____

C

Write true, false, or maybe.

> **Here's the only thing Mary did.**
> **Mary read some of the wide books.**

① ② ③ ④

1. Mary read object 1. _____

2. Mary read object 3. _____

3. Mary did not read object 4. _____

D

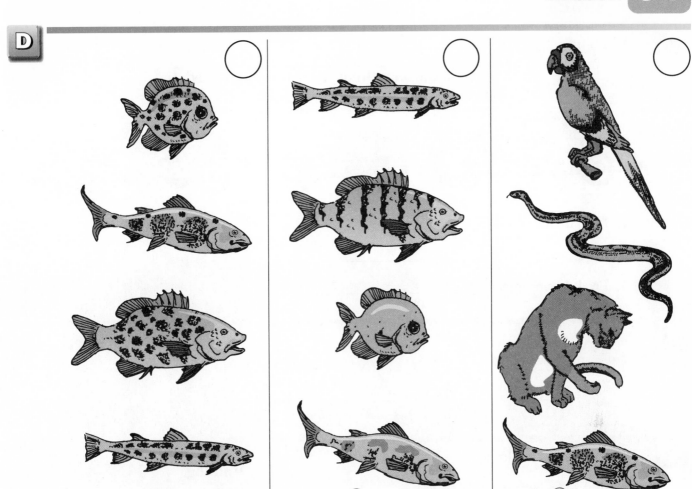

_____ _____

animals   spotted fish   fish

E

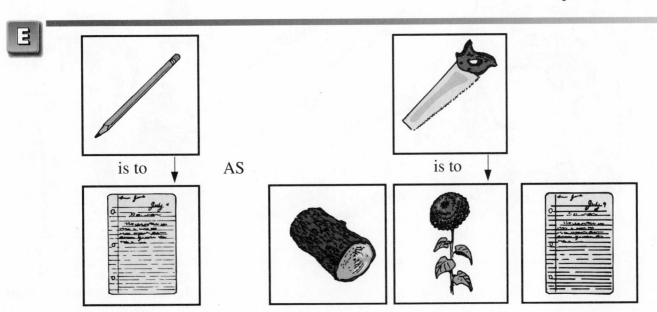

is to ↓   AS   is to ↓

1	2	3	4

TOTAL

A

Write true, false, or maybe.

> **Here's the only thing we know about Fred.**
> **Fred did not drive the long cars.**

① ② ③

1. Fred drove object 3. _____

2. Fred drove object 2. _____

3. Fred drove object 1. _____

B

① ② ③ ④ ⑤

C

Complete the analogy.

A bird is to flying as a fish is to _____.

walking
swimming
talking

D

 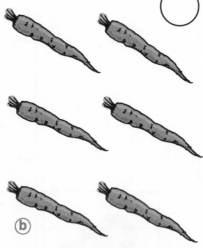 

ⓐ _____ ⓑ _____ ⓒ _____

living things   carrots   plants

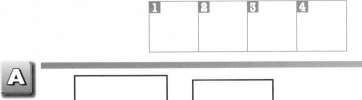

LESSON 36

A

① ② ③ ④ ⑤

B Write true, false, or maybe.

Here's the only thing we know about Tom.
Tom did not write with the fat pencils.

① ② ③ ④

1. Tom wrote with object 1. _____

2. Tom wrote with object 2. _____

3. Tom wrote with object 3. _____

C Complete the analogy.

A man is to a hand as a bear is to a _____.

tail
head
paw

D

ⓐ ⓑ ⓒ

_____

animals   dogs   living things

1	2	3	4		TOTAL

A

①   ②   ③   ④

——— ——— ——— ———

——— ——— ——— ———

——— ——— ——— ———

B Write true, false, or maybe.

> **Here's the only thing we know about Jane.**
> **Jane did not swing the black bats.**

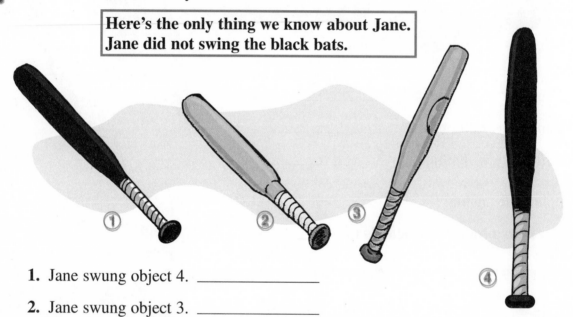

1. Jane swung object 4. ——————

2. Jane swung object 3. ——————

3. Jane swung object 2. ——————

C

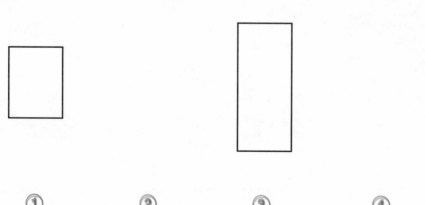

①   ②   ③   ④   ⑤

D

ⓐ _____

ⓑ _____

ⓒ _____

shoes   objects   clothing

E

Complete the analogy.

A pencil is to wood as a nail is to _____.

metal
plastic
paper

1	2	3	4		TOTAL

A

① ② ③ ④

___ ___ ___ ___

___ ___ ___ ___

___ ___ ___ ___

B

① ② ③ ④ ⑤

C

Grass is to short as a tree is to _____.

fat
tall
short

D

ⓐ ⓑ ⓒ

_____ _____ _____

containers   cups   objects

E

ⓐ ⓑ ⓒ ⓓ

1. ___

2. ___

3. ___

1	2	3	4

TOTAL

A

① ② ③ ④ ⑤

B

① ② ③ ④ ⑤

____ ____ ____ ____ ____

____ ____ ____ ____ ____

____ ____ ____ ____ ____

____ ____ ____ ____ ____

C

A hammer is to tools as meat is to _____.

food
red
soft

D

ⓐ ⓑ ⓒ ⓓ

1. _____
2. _____
3. _____

A

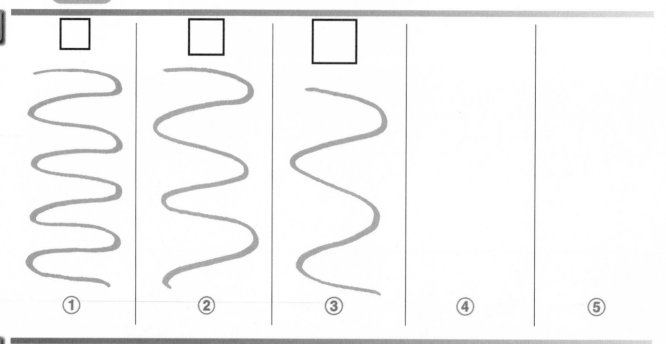

①   ②   ③   ④   ⑤

B

Write true, false, or maybe.

> **Here's the only thing John did.**
> **John planted some tall trees.**

① ② ③ ④

1. John planted object 3. _____

2. John did not plant object 1. _____

3. John planted object 2. _____

A

① ② ③ ④ ⑤

B

ⓐ   ⓑ   ⓒ

_____   _____   _____

containers   objects   glasses

C

Write true, false, or maybe.

> **Here's the only thing Terry did.**
> **Terry made some of the small bowls.**

① ② ③ ④

1. Terry made object 4.   _____

2. Terry made object 2.   _____

3. Terry did not make object 3. _____

D

Book is to paper as car is to _____ .

paper
plastic
metal

E

1. Pass   Fail

F

1. Pass   Fail   **3.** Pass   Fail

2. Pass   Fail   **4.** Pass   Fail

1	2	3	4		TOTAL

A

 ① ②  ③ ④  ⑤

_____   _____   _____   _____   _____

_____   _____   _____   _____   _____

_____   _____   _____   _____   _____

B

10 | 9 | 8 | | |
① | ② | ③ | ④ | ⑤

C

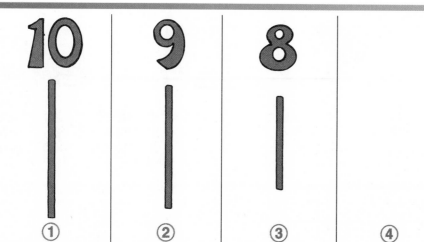

① ② ③

1. While the bell was ringing, a woman brushed her hair.
2. While the bell was ringing, a woman read a book.
3. While the bell was ringing, a woman touched her toes.

D

A truck is to vehicles as a dog is to _____.

animals
food
tools

E

ⓐ ⓑ ⓒ ⓓ

1. _____
2. _____
3. _____

1	2	3	4

TOTAL

A

① ② ③ ④ ⑤

_____ _____ _____ _____ _____

_____ _____ _____ _____ _____

_____ _____ _____ _____ _____

_____

B

1. While the fire was burning, a man wore a coat.
2. While the fire was burning, a man chopped wood.
3. While the fire was burning, a man wore a hat.

C

① ② ③ ④ ⑤

D

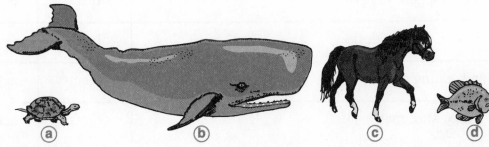

1. _____
2. _____
3. _____

1	2	3	4		TOTAL

A

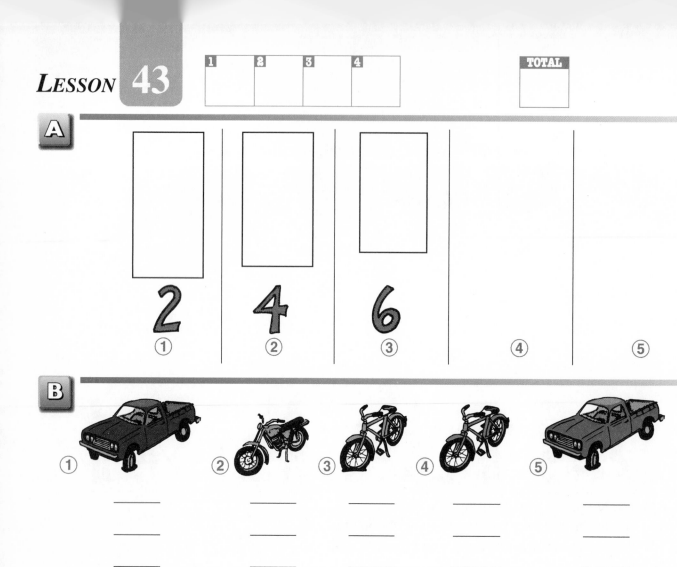

B

C

1. When the line is long, the circle is starred.
2. When the line is long, the circle is big.
3. When the line is long, the circle is small.

D

1.	Ball, elephant, man, sister, cup	objects	actions
2.	sleeping, run, stopped, jumping	objects	actions
3.	book, paper, car, giraffe, desk	objects	actions
4.	sitting, stand, eating a pear	objects	actions
5.	hiding in a box, slid, masticate	objects	actions

A

①	②	③	④
X	X	X	X
Z	K	D	Z
D	T	R	T
K	R	E	E

B

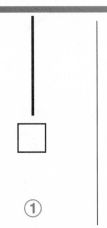 

①   ②   ③   ④   ⑤

C

1. dog, book, bike, sheep, table	objects	actions
2. watching, drink, breathe, talk, destroying	objects	actions
3. clocks, deck of cards, bottle, bear	objects	actions
4. rat, sidewalk, store, city, park	objects	actions
5. driving, wiggling, dancing on a table	objects	actions

D

1. When the square is striped, the triangle is little.
2. When the square is striped, the triangle is large.
3. When the square is striped, the triangle is dotted.

1	2	3	4

TOTAL

A

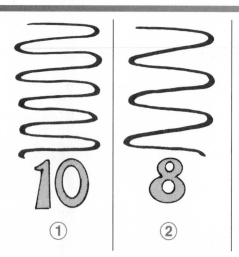

① ② ③ ④ ⑤

___ ___ ___ ___ ___

___ ___ ___ ___ ___

___ ___ ___ ___ ___

___ ___ ___ ___ ___

B

① ② ③ ④ ⑤

C

1. standing on your head, slipping, snoring	objects	actions
2. shoes, truck, pants, box, pen	objects	actions
3. lighting a match, ignore, chew	objects	actions
4. yelling, singing a song, read	objects	action
5. football, towel, glass, magazine	objects	actions

D

1. Each time the cow was in the barn, it ate hay.
2. Each time the cow was in the barn, it mooed.
3. Each time the cow was outside, it ate hay.

A

① ② ③ ④ ⑤

①	②	③	④	⑤
B	B	B	B	B
C	D	C	C	D
F	F	A	F	A
G	E	H	G	E
E			E	

B

① ② ③ ④ ⑤

C

1. desk, squirrel, balloon, bag, lion	objects	actions
2. sleep, watching, throw, drop	objects	actions
3. chew, study, see, typing	objects	actions
4. scratching, amble, traveling on a bus	objects	actions
5. hamburger, jacket, newspaper, rug, bug	objects	actions

D

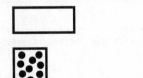

1. When the rectangle is long, the circle is dotted.
2. When the rectangle is dotted, the circle is big.
3. When the rectangle is short, the square is dotted.

1	2	3	4		TOTAL

A

1. When the moon was half full, the tiger roared.
2. When the moon was half full, the tiger chased a butterfly.
3. When the moon was half full, the tiger drank from a river.

B

ⓐ   ⓑ   ⓒ

_____ _____

human beings   women   mammals

C

A pen is to writing as a knife is to _____.
     blade
     handle
     cutting

D

1. reading, wearing a coat, descend, go	objects	actions
2. drinking coffee, pull, fall, seeing	objects	actions
3. coffee, bus, coats, airplane, sharks	objects	actions
4. talking, duplicate, sipping a milkshake	objects	actions
5. popcorn, milkshake, notebook, canine	objects	actions

E

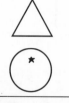

1	2	3	4

A

①  ②  ③  ④  ⑤

_____ _____ _____ _____ _____

_____ _____ _____ _____ _____

_____ _____ _____ _____ _____

_____

B

1. When the line is wavy, the glass is full.
2. When the line is straight, the glass is empty.
3. When the line is straight, the glass is full.

C

	objects	actions
1. telephone, dress, car, butterfly, bus	objects	actions
2. talking on a telephone, eating, riding	objects	actions
3. skated, sit, breathe	objects	actions
4. stand up, clean, paddle	objects	actions
5. machine, wagon, cat, pencil, chair	objects	actions

D

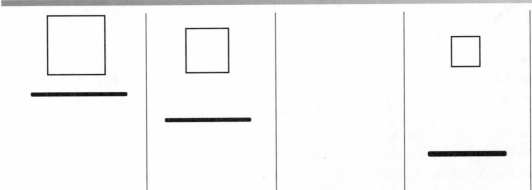

1	2	3	4		TOTAL

A

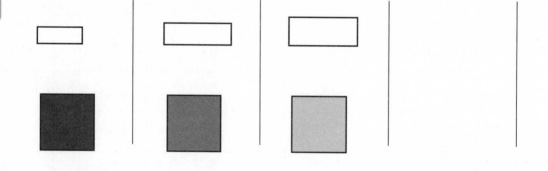

①	②	③	④	⑤	⑥
Z	Z	Z	Z	Z	Z
X	V	Y	Y	Y	Y
T	T	W	W	V	X

B

1. candy, factory, garage, potatoes, bike	objects	actions
2. eat potatoes, sit down, comprehend	objects	actions
3. typing, traveling in a car, swallow	objects	actions
4. move, look, chew, modify	objects	actions
5. hot dog, hat, floor, ship, pen	objects	actions

C

D

1. When the X is big, the big star is dotted.
2. When the X is small, the star is dotted.
3. When the X is big, the stars are big.

1. stretch, listen, consume | objects | actions | tell what kind
2. milk, player, giraffe | objects | actions | tell what kind
3. blue, sleepy, skinny | objects | actions | tell what kind
4. blow, slurp, hear | objects | actions | tell what kind
5. sewing, pull, drive | objects | actions | tell what kind

1. stretch, listen, consume	objects	actions	tell what kind
2. milk, player, giraffe	objects	actions	tell what kind
3. blue, sleepy, skinny	objects	actions	tell what kind
4. blow, slurp, hear	objects	actions	tell what kind
5. sewing, pull, drive	objects	actions	tell what kind

Underline the carnivorous animals.
Circle the herbivorous animals.

LESSON 50

A

1.	chair, elephant, pencil, motorcycle	objects	actions
2.	frog, television, pillow, woman	objects	actions
3.	hop, leap, masticate, cry	objects	actions
4.	amble, smile, yell, kick	objects	actions
5.	bowl, book, letter, ladder	objects	actions

B

① ② ③ ④ ⑤

C

1. When the line is long, the square is big.
2. When the line is straight, the square is big.
3. When the line is straight, the square is small.

D

1. Pass   Fail

E

1. Pass   Fail

2. Pass   Fail

3. Pass   Fail

F

1. Pass   Fail

A

1. When it was spring, the bear slept.
2. When it was spring, the bear ate a fish.
3. When it was winter, the bear slept.

B

1. wear, pick, cough	objects	actions	tell what kind
2. wet, loud, indolent	objects	actions	tell what kind
3. boil, roar, inquire	objects	actions	tell what kind
4. insect, paper clip, jacket	objects	actions	tell what kind
5. mouse, grass, jar	objects	actions	tell what kind

C

Wet is to dry as full is to _____.

quiet
long
empty

D

Write true, false, or maybe.

> **Here's the only thing we know about Max.**
> **Max chewed none of the small bones.**

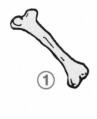

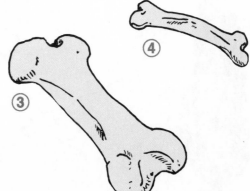

1. Max chewed object 1. _____

2. Max chewed object 3. _____

3. Max chewed object 4. _____

1	2	3	4

TOTAL

A

Write true, false, or maybe.

> **Here's the only thing Sue did.**
> **Sue wore some of the white shirts.**

① ② ③ ④ ⑤

1. Sue wore object 1. _____

2. Sue did not wear object 3. _____

3. Sue wore object 4. _____

B

	objects	actions	tell what kind
1. motorcycle, ink, lamp	objects	actions	tell what kind
2. hot, sticky, lumpy	objects	actions	tell what kind
3. skates, water, picture	objects	actions	tell what kind
4. mean, happy, quick	objects	actions	tell what kind
5. envelope, flower, shell	objects	actions	tell what kind

C

Christmas is to December as Independence Day is to _____.

June
January
July

D

ⓐ ⓑ ⓒ ⓓ

1. _____
2. _____
3. _____

A

① ② ③ ④ ⑤

___ ___ ___ ___ ___

___ ___ ___ ___ ___

___ ___ ___ ___ ___

B

			objects	actions	tell what kind
1.	furry, tall, round		objects	actions	tell what kind
2.	clock, rock, ashes		objects	actions	tell what kind
3.	terrible, glad, sloppy		objects	actions	tell what kind
4.	read, carry, complete		objects	actions	tell what kind
5.	deduce, touch, shut		objects	actions	tell what kind

C

Write true, false, or maybe.

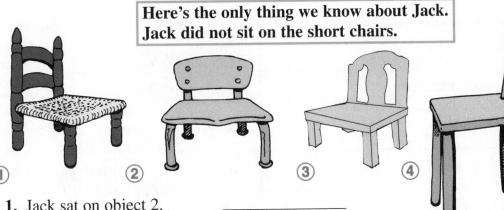

Here's the only thing we know about Jack.
Jack did not sit on the short chairs.

① ② ③ ④

1. Jack sat on object 2. _____

2. Jack did not sit on object 3. _____

3. Jack sat on object 4. _____

D

Winter is to cold as summer is to _____.

dry
hot
cold

1	2	3	4		TOTAL

A

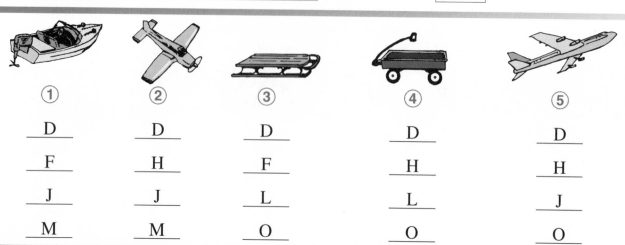

① ② ③ ④ ⑤

D	D	D	D	D
F	H	F	H	H
J	J	L	L	J
M	M	O	O	O

B

People are to skin as trees are to _____.   bark   skin   green

C

Write true, false, or maybe.

> **Here's the only thing Cleo will do.**
> **Cleo will wash some of the dirty plates.**

① ② ③ ④

1. Cleo will wash object 2.   _____

2. Cleo will wash object 4.   _____

3. Cleo will wash object 1.   _____

D

1. dirty, broken, clean	objects	actions	tell what kind
2. clouds, man, mountain	objects	actions	tell what kind
3. flying, sweep, pour	objects	actions	tell what kind
4. hit, fishing, weep	objects	actions	tell what kind
5. leaves, pins, card	objects	actions	tell what kind

E

Make a box around the herbivorous animals.
Circle the carnivorous animals.

    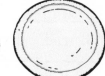

1	2	3	4

TOTAL

A

a

b

c

_____   _____   house cats   felines   mammals

B

1. bounce, catch, run	objects	actions	tell what kind
2. cut, watering, spin	objects	actions	tell what kind
3. pretty, yellow, quiet	objects	actions	tell what kind
4. destroy, complete, masticate	objects	actions	tell what kind
5. indolent, weak, green	objects	actions	tell what kind

C

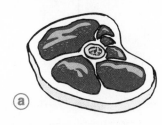

a   b   c   d

1. _____
2. _____
3. _____

D

Write true, false, or maybe.

> **Here's the only thing Bob did.**
> **Bob tore the spotted pants.**

① ② ③ ④

1. Bob tore object 3.   _____

2. Bob tore object 1.   _____

3. Bob did not tear object 4.   _____

1	2	3	4		TOTAL

A

A snake is to reptiles as an eagle is to _____.

mammals
reptiles
birds

B

1. ignore, amble, descend	objects	actions	tell what kind
2. canine, purse, plant	objects	actions	tell what kind
3. runny, difficult, silly	objects	actions	tell what kind
4. modify, leap, instruct	objects	actions	tell what kind
5. feline, containers, tree	objects	actions	tell what kind

C

Write true, false, or maybe.

> Here's the only thing the goat will do.
> The goat will eat some cans.

 ① ②  ③ 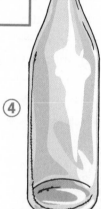 ④

1. The goat will eat object 1. _____

2. The goat will eat object 4. _____

3. The goat will not eat object 1. _____

D

ⓐ   ⓑ   ⓒ   ⓓ

1. _____

2. _____

3. _____

1	2	3	4

TOTAL

A Write true, false, or maybe.

> **Here's the only thing we know about Judy.**
> **Judy rode none of the black horses.**

1. Judy rode object 2. _____

2. Judy did not ride object 1. _____

3. Judy rode object 4. _____

B

1. obtain, duplicate, examine	objects	actions	tell what kind
2. large, funny, wild	objects	actions	tell what kind
3. comprehend, exhibit, inquire	objects	actions	tell what kind
4. shiny, dull, striped	objects	actions	tell what kind
5. construct, consume, complete	objects	actions	tell what kind

C Make a C on the carnivorous animals.
Make an H on the herbivorous animals.

D **A trout is to fish as a bat is to _____.**

birds
mammals
reptiles

E

1. _____
2. _____
3. _____

1	8	3	4		TOTAL

A

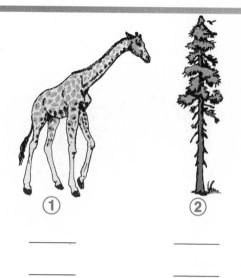

① ② ③ ④

_____ _____ _____ _____

_____ _____ _____ _____

_____ _____ _____ _____

B

A leopard is to spots as a zebra is to _____.   stripes
dots
checks

C

	objects	actions	tell what kind
1. vehicles, appliance, animal	objects	actions	tell what kind
2. pitcher, stove, bread	objects	actions	tell what kind
3. climb, shout, spell	objects	actions	tell what kind
4. thin, purple, plastic	objects	actions	tell what kind
5. real, hard, soft	objects	actions	tell what kind

D

Write true, false, or maybe.

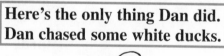

Here's the only thing Dan did.
Dan chased some white ducks.

① ② ③ ④

1. Dan chased object 3. _____

2. Dan did not chase object 2. _____

3. Dan chased object 1. _____

1	2	3	4

TOTAL

A

① ② ③ ④ ⑤

C	C	C	C	C
E	E	G	E	G
J	I	J	I	J
L		L		

B

1. lizard, bat, trunk	objects	actions	tell what kind
2. sprinkle, swim, shoot	objects	actions	tell what kind
3. healthy, slick, dry	objects	actions	tell what kind
4. exhibit, bush, tiger	objects	actions	tell what kind
5. deduce, decrease, dig	objects	actions	tell what kind

C

Write true, false, or maybe.

> **Here's the only thing Meg did.**
> **Meg dug some deep holes.**

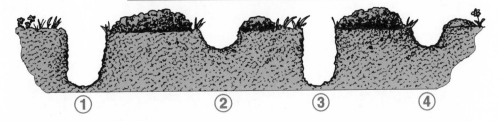

① ② ③ ④

1. Meg did not dig object 1. _____

2. Meg dug object 3. _____

3. Meg dug object 4. _____

D

A lion is to carnivorous as a gorilla is to _____.

herbivorous
canine
amphibian

A

1. deep, lucky, smooth	objects	actions	tell what kind
2. elephant, dish, train	objects	actions	tell what kind
3. masticate, instruct, comprehend	objects	actions	tell what kind
4. television, fireplace, airplane	objects	actions	tell what kind
5. wall, bucket, goat	objects	actions	tell what kind

B

Write true, false, or maybe.

> **Here's the only thing Nan did.**
> **Nan dropped some small cups.**

1   2   3   4

1. Nan dropped object 2. _____

2. Nan dropped object 1. _____

3. Nan dropped object 3. _____

TOTAL

A

1. shiny, long, fat	objects	actions	tell what kind
2. flower, canine, bike	objects	actions	tell what kind
3. blanket, street, purse	objects	actions	tell what kind
4. modify, run, sew	objects	actions	tell what kind
5. dull, indolent, striped	objects	actions	tell what kind

B

Cross out the carnivorous animals.
Circle the herbivorous animals.

C

1. _____
2. _____
3. _____

D

①	②	③	④	⑤
R	R	R	R	R
T	X	T	T	X
M	A	M	A	M
C	B	B	C	C

E

1. Pass   Fail   2. Pass   Fail   3. Pass   Fail

F

1. Pass   Fail   2. Pass   Fail   3. Pass   Fail

REMEDIATION AND REVIEW EXERCISES
FOR TEST 1
(Lesson 20)

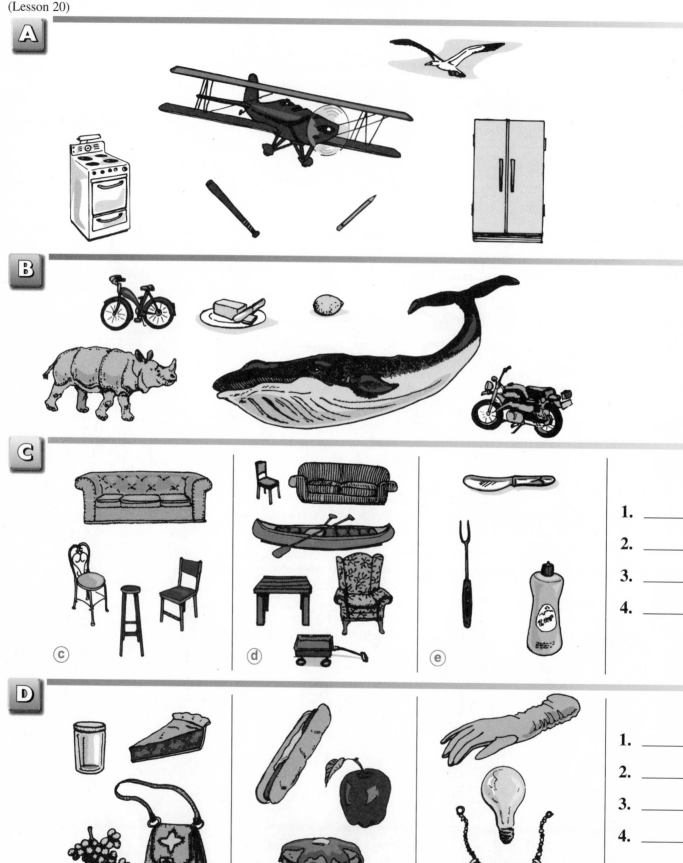

E

① ② ③

F

① ② ③

G

1. true false maybe
2. true false maybe
3. true false maybe
4. true false maybe

H

1. true false maybe
2. true false maybe
3. true false maybe
4. true false maybe

REMEDIATION AND REVIEW EXERCISES FOR TEST 2

(Lesson 30)

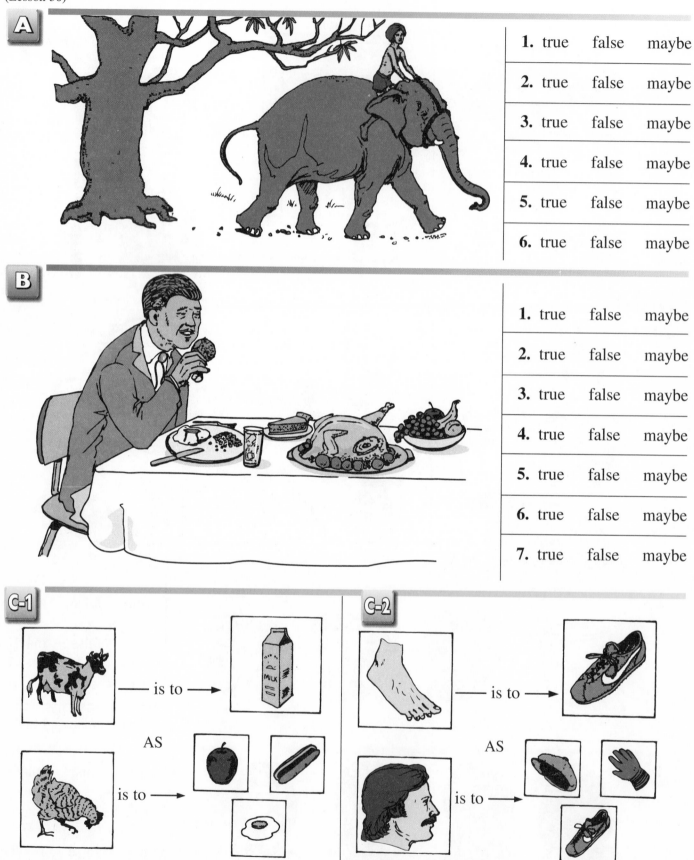

A

1. true	false	maybe
2. true	false	maybe
3. true	false	maybe
4. true	false	maybe
5. true	false	maybe
6. true	false	maybe

B

1. true	false	maybe
2. true	false	maybe
3. true	false	maybe
4. true	false	maybe
5. true	false	maybe
6. true	false	maybe
7. true	false	maybe

C-1

is to ——→

AS

is to ——→

C-2

is to ——→

AS

is to ——→

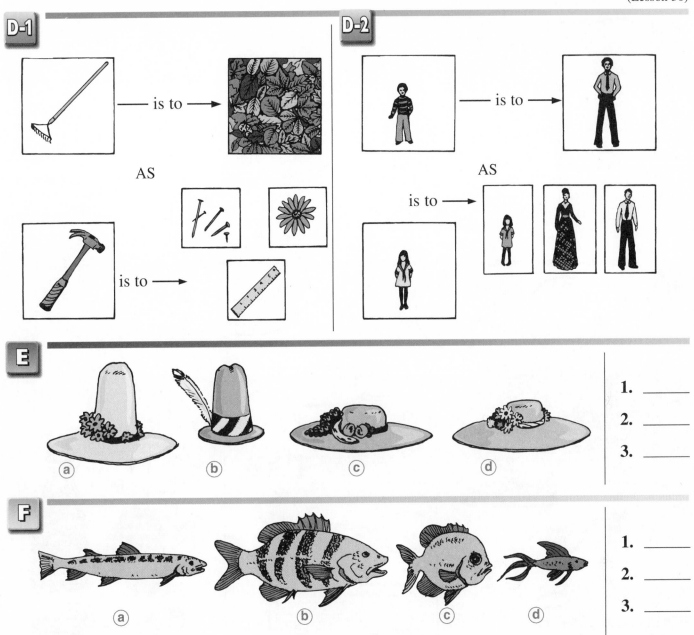

D-1

rake is to leaves

AS

hammer is to → [ruler]

D-2

boy is to man

AS

is to →

girl

E

a   b   c   d

1. ____
2. ____
3. ____

F

a   b   c   d

1. ____
2. ____
3. ____

REMEDIATION AND REVIEW EXERCISES
FOR TEST 3
(Lesson 40)

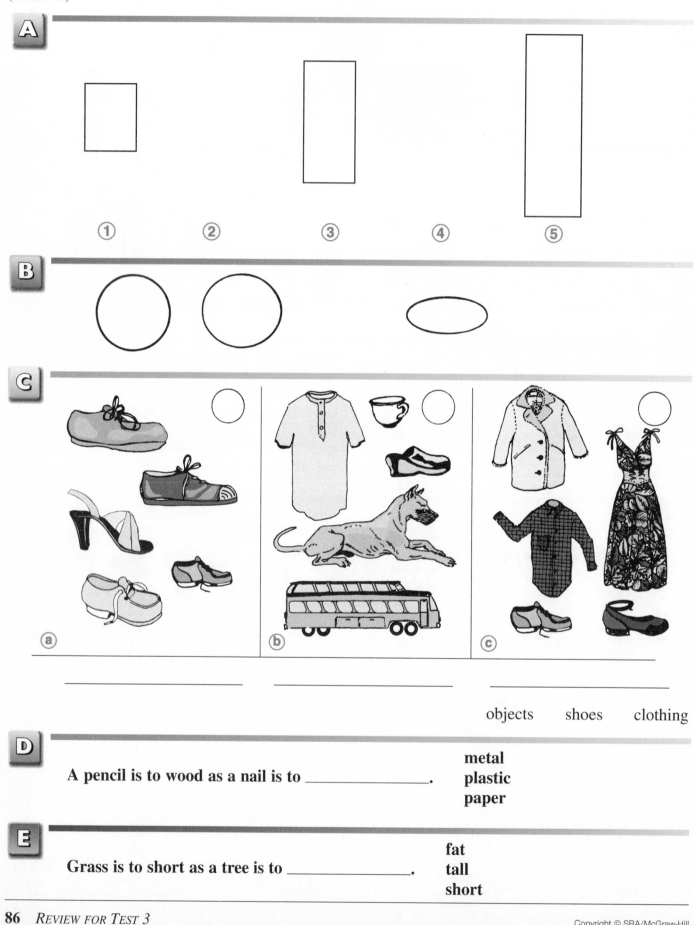

A

① ② ③ ④ ⑤

B

C

ⓐ ⓑ ⓒ

objects   shoes   clothing

D

A pencil is to wood as a nail is to _____.

metal
plastic
paper

E

Grass is to short as a tree is to _____.

fat
tall
short

a	b	c

_____   _____   _____

containers   cups   objects

 G

Here's the only thing we know about Tom. Tom did not write with the fat pencils.

1. Tom wrote with object 1. _____

2. Tom wrote with object 2. _____

3. Tom wrote with object 3. _____

H

Here's the only thing we know about Jane. Jane did not swing the black bats.

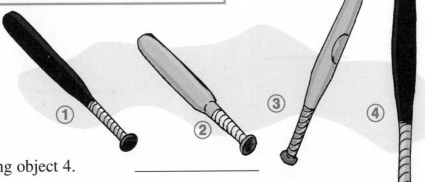

1. Jane swung object 4. _____

2. Jane did not swing object 3. _____

3. Jane swung object 2. _____

REMEDIATION AND REVIEW EXERCISES FOR TEST 4

(Lesson 50)

A

1. reading, wearing a coat, descend, go	objects	actions
2. drinking coffee, pull, fall, seeing	objects	actions
3. coffee, bus, coats, airplane, sharks	objects	actions
4. talking, duplicate, sipping a milkshake	objects	actions
5. popcorn, milkshake, notebook, canine	objects	actions

B

1. telephone, dress, car, butterfly, bus	objects	actions
2. talking on a telephone, eating, riding	objects	actions
3. skated, sit, breathe	objects	actions
4. stand up, clean, paddle	objects	actions
5. machine, wagon, cat, pencil, chair	objects	actions

C

D

E

1. When the moon was half full, the tiger roared.
2. When the moon was half full, the tiger chased a butterfly.
3. When the moon was half full, the tiger drank from a river.

F

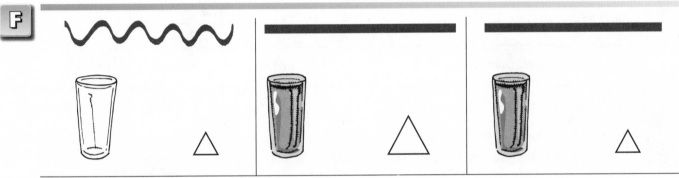

1. When the line is wavy, the glass is full.
2. When the line is straight, the glass is empty.
3. When the line is straight, the glass is full.

REMEDIATION AND REVIEW EXERCISES
FOR TEST 5
(Lesson 60)

 A

1. obtain, duplicate, examine	objects	actions	tell what kind
2. large, funny, wild	objects	actions	tell what kind
3. comprehend, exhibit, inquire	objects	actions	tell what kind
4. shiny, dull, striped	objects	actions	tell what kind
5. construct, consume, complete	objects	actions	tell what kind

B

1. vehicles, appliance, animal	objects	actions	tell what kind
2. pitcher, stove, bread	objects	actions	tell what kind
3. climb, shout, spell	objects	actions	tell what kind
4. thin, purple, plastic	objects	actions	tell what kind
5. real, hard, soft	objects	actions	tell what kind

C

Make a box around the herbivorous animals.
Circle the carnivorous animals.

 D

Make a C on the carnivorous animals.
Make an H on the herbivorous animals.

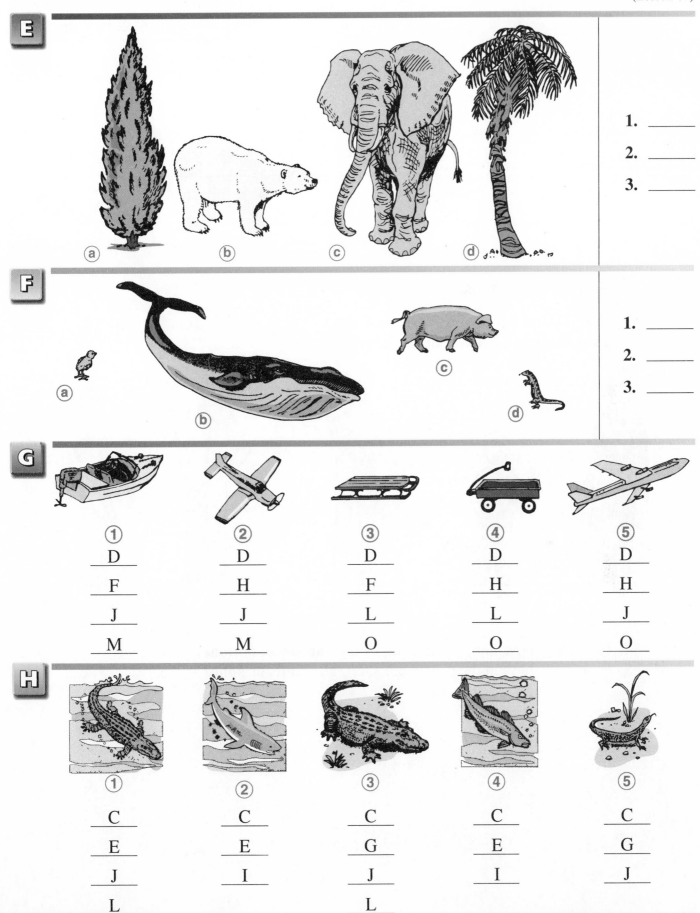

E

(a) (b) (c) (d)

1. ____
2. ____
3. ____

F

(a) (b) (c) (d)

1. ____
2. ____
3. ____

G

① D F J M
② D H J M
③ D F L O
④ D H L O
⑤ D H J O

H

① C E J L
② C E I L
③ C G J L
④ C E I
⑤ C G J

FACT GAME LESSON

1

(AFTER LESSON E)

FACT GAME SCORECARD

1	2	3	4	5	6	7	8	9	10
11	12	13	14	15	16	17	18	19	20
21	22	23	24	25	26	27	28	29	30

1. How are objects 1 and 2 the same?

① ② ③ ④

2. How are objects 1 and 3 the same?

3. Here's a rule. **All the boys are standing**.
Does that rule tell about all the pictures?

4. How many boys in the picture are sitting, **all, some,** or **none?**
5. How many boys in the picture are short, **all, some,** or **none?**

6. Here's the rule.
All the glass doors have a lion behind them.
Does that rule tell about object 1?

FACT GAME
LESSON

2

1	2	3	TOTAL

1	2	3	4	5	6	7	8	9	10
11	12	13	14	15	16	17	18	19	20
21	22	23	24	25	26	27	28	29	30

1. How many months are in a year?
2. What does **obtain** mean?
3. Name the class these objects are in.
   Bus, boat, wagon, jet, bike.
4. How are a red house and a blue house the same?
5. How are a hammer and a saw the same?
6. All dogs bark. Collies are dogs.
   So, _____.

 A

Circle the containers.
Cross out the vehicles.

B

C

| **1.** true   false | **2.** true   false | **3.** true   false | **4.** true   false |

D

① ② ③

E

ⓐ ⓑ ⓒ

1. _____

2. _____

3. _____

1		2		3		TOTAL

FACT GAME SCORECARD

1	2	3	4	5	6	7	8	9	10
11	12	13	14	15	16	17	18	19	20
21	22	23	24	25	26	27	28	29	30

1. What season comes after spring?
2. Name the seasons of the year.
3. What's a synonym for **indolent?**
4. Figure out the class of animals.
   These animals are cold-blooded and are born on land.
5. Snakes don't walk. Cobras are snakes.
   So, _____.
6. Here's a rule. **All boys eat.**
   Say the rule with **every.**

A

1. true	false	maybe
2. true	false	maybe
3. true	false	maybe
4. true	false	maybe
5. true	false	maybe

B

Circle the tools.
Cross out the buildings.

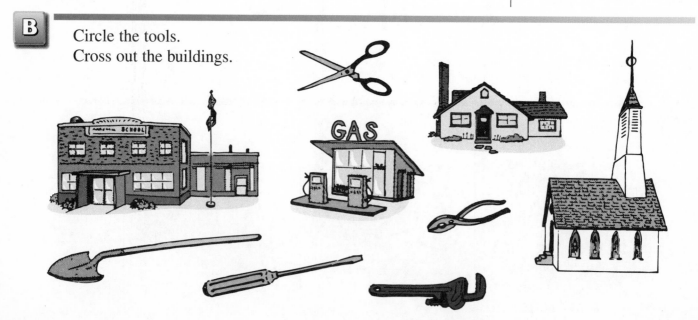

C

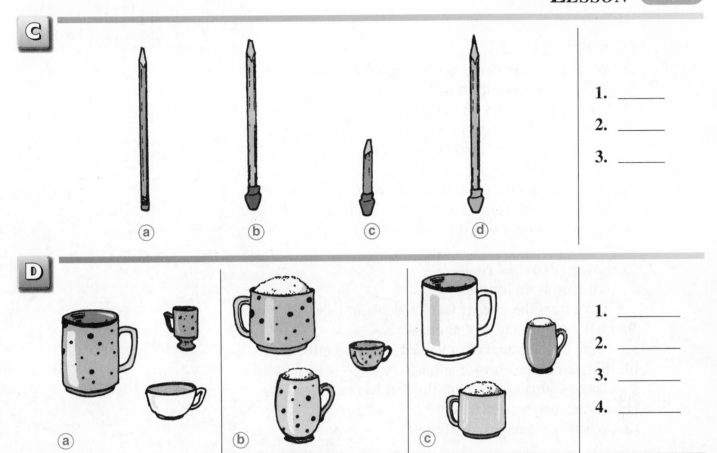

1. _____
2. _____
3. _____

ⓐ ⓑ ⓒ ⓓ

D

ⓐ ⓑ ⓒ

1. _____
2. _____
3. _____
4. _____

4

| 1 | | 2 | | 3 | | TOTAL |

FACT GAME SCORECARD

1	2	3	4	5	6	7	8	9	10
11	12	13	14	15	16	17	18	19	20
21	22	23	24	25	26	27	28	29	30

2. What are all members of the dog family called?

3. What does **descend** mean?

4. What's a synonym for **jump?**

5. Figure out the class of animals.
   These animals are cold-blooded and are born
   in water and grow up on land.

6. **Dogs don't have gills. Poodles are dogs.**
   What does the rule let you know about poodles?

7. Some girls wear glasses. Jane is a girl.
   So, _____.

8. **Every plant has roots.**
   An emu is an animal.
   What does the rule let you know about an emu?

9. Figure out the class of animals.
   These animals are cold-blooded and have gills.

10. Figure out the class of animals.
    These animals are warm-blooded and have feathers.

11. What's a synonym for **cat?**

12. What's a synonym for **change?**

ⓐ   ⓑ   ⓒ

1. _____
2. _____
3. _____
4. _____

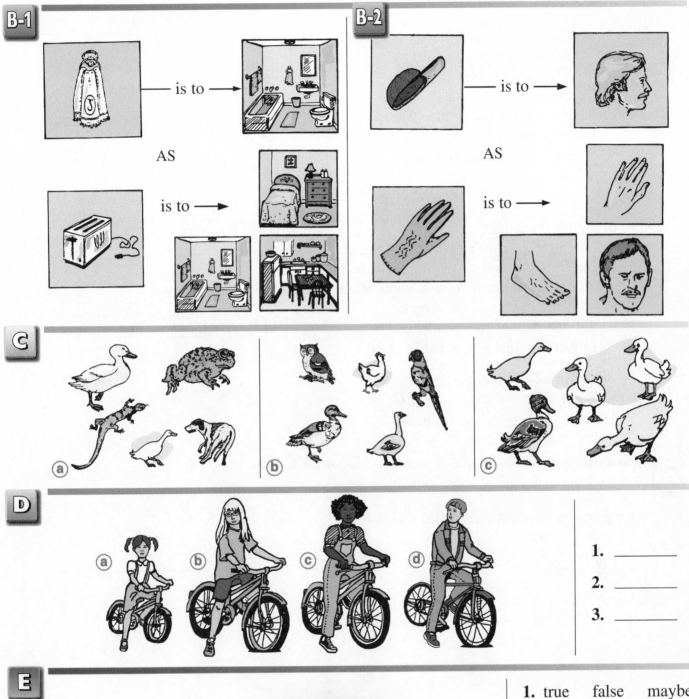

B-1

is to →

AS

is to →

B-2

is to →

AS

is to →

C

ⓐ   ⓑ   ⓒ

D

ⓐ   ⓑ   ⓒ   ⓓ

1. _____
2. _____
3. _____

E

1. true	false	maybe
2. true	false	maybe
3. true	false	maybe
4. true	false	maybe
5. true	false	maybe
6. true	false	maybe

1		2		3		TOTAL

FACT GAME SCORECARD

1	2	3	4	5	6	7	8	9	10
11	12	13	14	15	16	17	18	19	20
21	22	23	24	25	26	27	28	29	30

2. What's a synonym for **big?**
3. Tell the date of New Year's Day.
4. What's a synonym for **healthy?**
5. Listen to this deduction.
   Some animals fly.
   A dolphin is an animal.

   So, _____.
   Say the whole deduction.
6. Finish this analogy.
   Skinny is to thin as under is to _____.
7. **No fish have hair. A salmon is a fish.**
   What does the rule let you know about a salmon?
8. What's a synonym for **wreck?**
9. Tell the date of Independence Day.
10. Finish this analogy. **A robin is to**

    flying as a fish is to _____.
11. What's a synonym for **fast?**
12. What word means **get bigger?**

A Complete the analogy.

A horse is to mammals as an owl is to _____.

fish

birds

reptiles

B

amphibians   frogs   animals

C

Write true, false, or maybe.

> **Here's the only thing the dog did.**
> **The dog ate some of the small bones.**

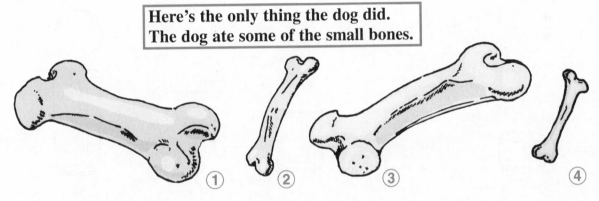

1. The dog ate object 1.   _____

2. The dog did not eat object 4.   _____

3. The dog ate object 2.   _____

D

1		2		3		TOTAL

1	2	3	4	5	6	7	8	9	10
11	12	13	14	15	16	17	18	19	20
21	22	23	24	25	26	27	28	29	30

2. What's the opposite of **outside?**
3. What word means **look at?**
4. What's the opposite of **young?**
5. Name the holiday that comes at the end of November.
6. What word means **eat** or **use up?**
7. Finish this analogy.
   Full is to empty as quiet is to _____.
8. Chair. **Object** or **action?**
9. What's a synonym for **understand?**
10. What's the opposite of **rough?**
11. Sitting on a chair. **Object** or **action?**
12. What's a synonym for **show?**

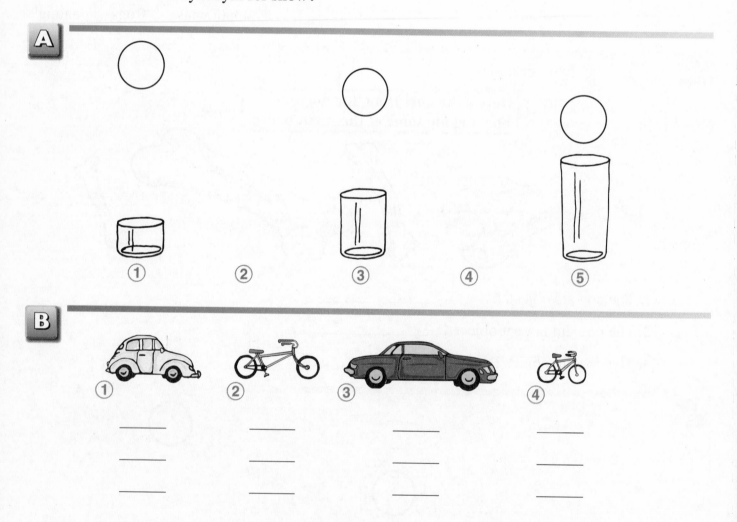

A

① ② ③ ④ ⑤

B

① ② ③ ④

C		objects	actions
1. cat, stove, jug of milk, pliers		objects	actions
2. obtain, riding a bike, sit, eating		objects	actions
3. pencils, cup, window, pair of shoes		objects	actions
4. drinking milk, modify, buying, instruct		objects	actions
5. swinging, write, sweep, cooking dinner		objects	actions

1. When it rained, the cat chased a bird.
2. When it rained, the cat climbed a tree.
3. When the sun was out, the cat climbed a tree.

1	2	3	TOTAL

FACT GAME SCORECARD

1	2	3	4	5	6	7	8	9	10
11	12	13	14	15	16	17	18	19	20
21	22	23	24	25	26	27	28	29	30

2. What word means **more than half?**
3. What's the opposite of **dangerous?**
4. What word means **figure out?**
5. What's the opposite of **push?**
6. What's a synonym for **ask?**
7. Some animals eat only plants.
   What are those animals called?
8. What's the opposite of **difficult?**
9. Some animals eat meat.
   What are those animals called?
10. What's the opposite of **soft?**
11. What word means **make** or **build?**
12. What's the opposite of **straight?**

Write true, false, or maybe.

> **Here's the only thing we know about the cat.**
> **The cat climbed none of the short trees.**

①   ②   ③   ④

1. The cat climbed object 4. _____

2. The cat climbed object 3. _____

3. The cat did not climbed object 2. _____

B

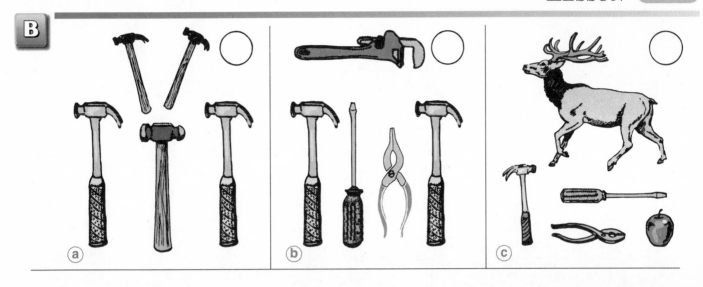

_____ _____ _____

tools   objects   hammers

C

1. _____
2. _____
3. _____

D

1. green, narrow, shiny	objects	actions	tell what kind
2. lose, start, descend	objects	actions	tell what kind
3. healthy, crooked, easy	objects	actions	tell what kind
4. basket, sun, door	objects	actions	tell what kind
5. destroy, weep, teach	objects	actions	tell what kind